Terrific Terrance's Team

Julia A. Royston

ROYSTON Publishing

BK Royston Publishing
P. O. Box 4321
Jeffersonville, IN 47131
502-802-5385
http://www.bkroystonpublishing.com
bkroystonpublishing@gmail.com

© Copyright – 2022

All Rights Reserved. No part of this book may be reproduced, stored in a retrieval system, or transmitted by any means without the written permission of the author.

Cover Design: Gad of Elite Book Covers

ISBN-13: 978-1-955063-73-9

Printed in the United States of America

Dedication

I dedicate this book to any person that doesn't feel special but with a friend who is a real friend, it is so much better and easier.

Let's go!

Acknowledgements

First, I acknowledge my Lord and Savior Jesus Christ for giving me all of my gifts and especially my gift to write His words.

My husband who is always supportive, loving and encouraging me to utilize all of my gifts and talents. Thank you honey.

To my mother, Dr. Daisy Foree, who is my number one cheerleader and always tells me, "hang in there, you can do it." To my father, Dr. Jack Foree, who is never far away from me in spirit or my heart. I only have to look in the mirror each day to see him.

To Rev. Claude and Mrs. Lillie Royston who support me in everything I do.

To the rest of my family, I love you and thank you for your prayers, support and love.

To the team of BK Royston Publishing and Royal Media and Publishing that make it easier for me to write and publish the books I love, thank you!

Table of Contents

Dedication   i
Acknowledgements   iii
Introduction   v

Candy Mystery Solved   **1**
Meeting with Ms. Wilson   **11**
In Trouble   **19**
Face the Music   **25**
Food, Tables and Trash Cans   **31**
The Right Way   **41**
Caught   **53**
We Survived 6th Grade   **69**
A Note from the Author   **83**
Questions for Discussion   **85**
About the Author   **87**

Introduction

If you read Book #1 and Book #2 of the Terrance the Terrific Series, I know that you are wondering exactly what happened with Terrance and Paris helping Roger find his missing candy. With those powerful eyes of Paris', it should have been quite easy to find. Right? Sure but with Darren always close by, who knows if the mystery will be solved and everything turn out alright.

So, let's turn the page and get the next installment of the Terrance the Terrific Series with Paris Carter who is now on Terrance's Team. Let's go!

Candy Mystery Solved

"Does everyone understand the assignment? Are there any questions?" Mr. Nelson, Terrance and Paris' math teacher, asked.

Neither Terrance nor Paris heard anything that Mr. Nelson had said prior to the assignment being given, but they were sure that they could figure it out. Terrance wrote down the assignment in his notebook but was packing up his books while still keeping his eyes on the clock.

When the bell rang, Terrance and Paris went straight into the hallway and met up with Roger.

"Roger, did you just have the candy still in the box or did you put it in something else?" Paris asked.

"I put it in my small yellow gym bag. I was going to put it in my locker, but it was stolen from me while I was in the bathroom. How low down is that?"

"I know, but did you see who took it?" Terrance asked.

"No, of course not," Roger said, quite irritated.

"You know who I suspect," Paris said.

"Yes, but we can't go on who we suspect. It has to be facts, Paris. We can't just go around accusing people," Terrance said.

"True, but it could help if I checked that locker first," Paris said.

"Good point," Terrance said.

"I don't care, just see if you can find it," Roger said.

"Okay," Paris replied.

The three of them walked down the hall toward a particular locker. When Paris put on her special pink glasses, she was able to see inside anything. She didn't put on her glasses until she was standing in front of the suspect locker a short walk down the hallway. When she stood in front of the locker and put on her glasses, she saw the yellow bag and the candy tucked away inside.

"This is it! I knew he took it!" Paris exclaimed.

"We don't see what you see, Paris, but are you sure that's it?" Terrance asked.

"Positive," Paris said.

"Okay, I am going to open it!" Terrance said as he reached for the handle and pulled on it. Nothing happened at first. Darren, Terrance's constant bully, laughed out loud at the failed attempt. No one else noticed because they were busy at their lockers.

Terrance heard him all right and remembered all of the other times he was teased by Darren. He also remembered how he felt when his super strength came upon him the last two times. He felt anger, fear and/or a combination of both. Terrance knew how much trouble he would be in, but he wanted to help someone who had been taken advantage of by the bully. This activated his anger. So when he pulled on the handle of the locker, not only did the locker door come open, but the entire locker came off the wall, door and all. The locker fell on the floor with a loud bang. It was noisy in the hallway, but all of the students stopped what they were doing to see what was going on and where the loud noise came from. It also wiped that grin and smug look off Darren's face. The entire hallway was a buzz of students saying, "Wow!" and "How did he do that?" or "What's going on with Terrance?"

Fortunately, just as Paris said, there was a yellow gym bag inside the locker with two boxes of candy inside.

"Is this it, Roger?" Paris asked with a smile.

"No, that's not mine," Roger said.

"It's a yellow gym bag with two boxes of candy inside, just like you said," Paris said.

"Yes, but my name, Roger, is going to be on the side in black permanent marker," Roger said.

"You never said that!" Paris yelled.

"So now, I'm in trouble for tearing off a locker that's not Darren's to get candy that not even yours!" Terrance exclaimed.

"I'm sorry. I forgot to tell you that part," Roger said sadly.

"That was a huge thing that you forgot, Roger," Paris said.

"I'm in big trouble because of you, Roger," Terrance continued.

"I'm sorry. I'm just trying to get my candy," Roger said with a whine.

"That won't help me now. I have to explain this!" Terrance exclaimed.

Just then, Kathy Booth walked up. "Why is my locker not even on the wall but on the ground?"

"I did that," Terrance admitted.

"You did that? How and why?" Kathy asked.

"I thought it was someone else's locker, and Roger said that someone stole his candy. Paris saw it and then I opened the locker. I was just trying to help," Terrance said.

"I now have to get a new locker, combination, and everything! Nothings seems to be missing, but, Terrance Edmonds, wait until I tell the principal!" Kathy yelled.

"Roger, now look what you've done!" Terrance said as he headed toward the office after Kathy.

"I'll go with you, Terrance. It's my fault, too. I didn't ask enough questions of Roger. Hopefully, Ms. Wilson will help us with the principal and help him to understand that we're both new to this helping people and stopping crime stuff anyway," Paris said.

"Mr. Smith won't understand anything, only Ms. Wilson," Terrance said.

"True," Paris replied.

"What can I do now? I still don't have my candy," Roger exclaimed.

"Nothing," Terrance and Paris said simultaneously.

On the other end of the hallway, Darren was just standing, staring at the entire scene, speechless.

Just then, Ms. Wilson came down the hallway. "What's going on here?"

"Ms. Wilson, Terrance tore my entire locker off the wall, supposedly looking for some stolen candy. I've got to tell Mr. Smith," Kathy said.

"Don't worry, Kathy, wait right here with me. I'll tell Mr. Smith and take care of getting you a new locker.

Terrance, Paris, and Roger, head to my office now. Everyone else, get to class. Everything is fine right here. Go around this locker mess and get to class," Ms. Wilson said. She then got on her walkie and called the head of maintenance.

The head of maintenance arrived and asked, "Ms. Wilson, who and how did they do this?"

"That's my job, Mr. Fleming, to find out. If you could get this cleaned up and find Kathy a new locker, I would greatly appreciate it.

"I'll try, but this is going to be a test of all of the lockers. Hopefully, the other lockers won't fall. The company is probably going to charge us for this."

"I know, but I'll take care of all of it, Mr. Fleming. If you could help Kathy get her things and assigned to a new locker, I would appreciate it. Kathy, come to my office and get a note to get into class when you're finished here," Ms. Wilson.

"Stand right here, Kathy, and I'll get you a box for your things," Mr. Fleming said, then went to get a box while Kathy watched over her things. What a day!

Meeting with Ms. Wilson

"I've never been in Ms. Wilson's office before," Roger said.

"Welcome," Terrance said. "I will probably be in here more now."

"Me, too," Paris said quietly.

Ms. Wilson's door opened and she stood there for a second, just looking at all three of them.

"I don't know where to start. I don't know whether I should start screaming and yelling or let Roger start talking and explain how we got here. Today is not a good day for any of you, but I'm going to stop myself long enough for all three of you to talk while I calm myself. Agreed?" Ms. Wilson asked.

"Agreed," they all three said.

"Roger, you start."

"I received my candy from homeroom but had to use the bathroom. I left it in homeroom. I was only gone a few minutes, but when I returned, the candy was gone," Roger said.

"Of course, it was, but I'll let you finish. What happened next?" Ms. Wilson asked.

"I told my homeroom teacher and she said go on to class. Terrance and Paris saw me in the hallway and asked me what was wrong. I told them, and after class, well, you know the rest," Roger continued.

"Yes, and Terrance and Paris are going to tell me the rest. What I want you to do now is go on to your next class. Here is a note. I'll have two more boxes of candy for you, so come straight to my office when the bell rings and before you get on the bus. Understand?" Ms. Wilson said.

"Yes, Ms. Wilson," Roger said as he took his note.

"Have a good rest of the day and close the door on your way out."

"Yes ma'am," Roger said.

"You're welcome, but if you lose or drop or leave or don't protect these two boxes of candy, it's on you. Understand?"

"Yes, Ms. Wilson."

Roger ran out of the office so fast that he forgot to close the door.

"Roger, the door!" Ms. Wilson reminded.

"I have it, Ms. Wilson. I'll close the door," Paris said as she jumped up to close the door.

"Yes, you will, young lady, and in a hurry, before I really blow my top."

"Listen, Ms. Wilson." Terrance began.

"No, you listen. You both are in huge trouble, but the original purpose for your powers is to help stop trouble and help others, not start trouble."

"It was my fault—," Paris began.

"Stop right there, before you go any further. On the other hand, it was really my fault because I haven't fully trained you on how to handle your super powers or what to do in a situation like this. It is really my fault. Agreed?"

"Agreed," Terrance and Paris said simultaneously."

"Ms. Wilson, can I say something?"

"Yes, Paris."

"I didn't ask enough questions of Roger. I told Terrance that it was that locker based on what he told me, and

Terrance took it off of the wall," Paris said.

"It wasn't just your fault, Paris, but mine as well. I should have never taken the locker off the wall, but I heard somebody laugh when the door didn't open at first. It made me mad and then, even stronger," Terrance said.

"Those are the kinds of things that I didn't tell you about. Controlling your emotions. Super powers or not, we all have to control our emotions in certain situations, or they will make us do things that we wouldn't normally do. Finally, with super powers, it is even more dangerous. Did you think about the people around you and if they could have gotten hurt, Terrance?" Ms. Wilson asked.

"No, ma'am."

"Of course not. You both just wanted to help, which is good, but, Terrance, you got angry when someone laughed at you on the first try at opening the locker. Am I right?"

"Yes, ma'am," Terrance and Paris said together again, with heads hanging down.

"Your help ended up destroying school property, which is terrible. Our next steps are for the property to be fixed, which I'll take care of because of my lack of instruction to you both. On the other hand, you'll have to be punished for your actions. Understand?"

"Yes, ma'am."

"Paris, you will have cafeteria duty for one week and, Terrance, starting tomorrow, you will work with the maintenance staff for one week, after school, because you live in the neighborhood. The week will end on next Tuesday. You will have detention the rest of this week and next Monday and Tuesday. Understand?"

"Yes, ma'am."

"Finally, when something arises where you think that you possibly will use your super powers, ask me first, and then I'll let you know if that is the best way to do it unless it just can't be helped. Understand?"

"Understand," they said together.

"I'll be calling your parents after this, and they'll be picking you up from school after we all have a conversation. Both of you report to this office immediately after the last class. In the meantime, here are notes for both of you to get into class. I haven't even looked at the clock to even know what class period it is.

"Third," Terrance said with a sigh.

"Thank you, and you both try to have a good rest of the day."

In Trouble

It doesn't matter how hard you try to explain it or think that it was a good idea, when you're in trouble, you're just in trouble. Terrance heard nothing that the teachers said from the second half of 3rd period until the end of the day. He and Paris ate lunch together, knowing that it would be their last lunch together for a long time. They didn't talk much because the cafeteria was all abuzz about what had happened earlier. The questions just kept coming, "Terrance, how did you tear that locker off of the wall?" to "Terrance, so now you are Terrance the Incredible or what?"

Sixth grade was hard enough without this added pressure. In Haven, Dr. Zoe had said that Terrance was chosen, but right now, he wanted to be unchosen, if that is a word.

"Will it ever stop, Paris?" Terrance asked between bites of his peanut butter and jelly sandwich with the crust taken off just the way he loved it.

"I don't know about anything stopping, Terrance, because each day, it keeps getting worse and worse. Speaking of worse, just wait until you are emptying trash cans after school and I am wiping down nasty middle school lunch trays for a week." Paris grimaced.

"Oh, Paris, that's going to be terrible. Maybe I am Terrance the Terrible like Darren has been saying all year."

"Take that back right now. You are not terrible. You are kind of terrific to me."

"Thanks, Paris." Terrance was so glad to be of darker skin so Paris couldn't see him blush or see his stomach was turning flip flops just realizing what Paris had just said.

They continued to walk down the hall toward class.

The other kids kind of stared and one commented, "There goes Superman now."

Another said, "He's able to take lockers off the wall with a single bound."

"No, that's Batman and Batgirl now."

"Ignore them, Terrance," Paris whispered.

"Trying, Paris, but it's not easy."

"They told us in Haven that we were chosen for this."

"Correct, but I don't like what goes along with being chosen."

"Me either, but hopefully, one day, it'll all make sense," Paris said.

"Hopefully," Terrence agreed.

They passed the row of lockers that now had a huge space where one was missing.

"Oh, wow, look how odd that looks," Paris said.

"Yeah, crazy that I can do that."

"Exactly, and I'm not putting my glasses on unless it's absolutely necessary. I don't want to see certain things."

"I agree."

"Well, I'm headed to art. See you after school, to face the music."

"Yep, it's graphic design for me so hopefully, I can focus. See you later, along with our parents."

"Good Luck."

"Right."

Face the Music

Like every kid in the world, Terrance and Paris were not ready to face their parents. Their hearts had been in the right place, but their actions didn't agree with the administrator or their parents.

"Terrance Edmonds, what did you do?" Mrs. Edmonds asked as soon as she opened the door of Ms. Wilson's office and headed toward the conference room table. Terrance and Paris were sitting across from each other. Mrs. Edmonds sat her purse on the table with a huff and Mr. Edmonds quietly sat down beside her. Paris waited because her parents hadn't arrived yet.

"Mom, I was trying to help—"

"Mrs. Edmonds, it was my fault, too," Paris interrupted.

"Paris, I love you, but I'm not your mother. Your mother will be here soon enough. I know you like my son, but don't try to take up for him, okay?" Mrs. Edmonds said as she rolled her eyes at Paris and turned back toward Terrance.

"Yes, ma'am," Paris said quietly.

"Terrance, explain," Mrs. Edmonds said.

Before Terrance could get the first word out, Paris' mother swung the door open. "Paris Queen Marie Carter! I left work early and there had better be a great reason! What is going on?"

Before Paris could respond, Ms. Wilson entered. "Good afternoon to you all, and I'm glad that you're all here. Please have a seat."

Ms. Wilson had her big flower on and the flower said, "Terrance is terrific and Paris has powerful eyes."

"Can you shut that flower of yours up?" Mrs. Carter asked.

"No, because he has something to say to you."

"Sleep, parents," the flower said, and the Edmonds and Mrs. Carter leaned back in the leather conference chairs and went to sleep immediately.

"Wow," Terrance and Paris both said.

"I need for them to hear clearly, get their emotions under control and realize what is going on here," Ms. Wilson said.

"If you say so, Ms. Wilson," Flower said.

"I say so. Flower, continue," Ms. Wilson answered.

"When you wake up, you will feel refreshed, your mind will be alert and you will be prepared, calm and ready to hear what happened to Terrance and Paris. Parents, awake," Flower ended and closed his petals.

The parents said nothing as Ms. Wilson explained everything that had happened.

When she ended the explanation, she asked, "Understand?"

The three parents answered in unison, "We understand."

"Great, take your children home and enjoy the rest of the evening. You will remember the conversation but with no anger toward your child," Ms. Wilson said and snapped her fingers.

The parents grabbed their belongings and headed toward the door.

"I wish I had that power all of the time," Paris whispered to Terrance.

"Me too. See you tomorrow," Terrance whispered back.

"Yeah, ready to report for cafeteria duty," Paris said sadly.

Surprisingly enough, when they got home, neither Terrance nor Paris' parents mentioned the meeting, the incident at school, or their detention punishment the entire evening. Miracle upon miracles, the incident appeared to have vanished into thin air. Neither Terrance nor Paris was convinced that things were over, but for now, there was peace and quiet in their respective houses.

Food, Tables, and Trash Cans

The next day when Terrance mother dropped him off to school, Darren was in his usual spot on the steps but said nothing to Terrance as he walked up the stairs. It was unusual, but Terrance was glad for once.

Ms. Wilson was standing in the hallway greeting the other students but saw Terrance and said, "Terrance, stop by my office after homeroom."

"Yes, ma'am," was Terrance's reply.

When Terrance arrived at his locker, Paris was already there, getting her books together.

"Hey," Terrance said.

"Hey, so you ready for this?" Paris asked.

"Ready as I'll ever be."

"Did Ms. Wilson see you?

"Yes, and she said to meet her in her office after homeroom."

"She told me that too. I wore my cafeteria duty clothes and shoes."

"You still look nice."

"Thanks. I had to be ready in case somebody accidentally missed the trash can and got food on me."

"Right. Well, I'll be emptying plenty of trash cans after school."

"Be careful and keep your eyes and ears open."

"Will do. You got everything?"

"Yes."

"Let's go."

Terrance and Paris had been in school together since 1st grade, so they knew each other rather well. Since their major issues at school, they had become closer friends than ever. Hopefully, this day would be okay and not be worse than the ones before.

Homeroom went without a problem, and then they both arrived in Ms. Wilson's office.

"There you two are. Mrs. Davies will be waiting for you in the cafeteria. You will help clean tables and empty trash for lunchtimes 1 and 2. I know that your lunch is 3, but you can eat during your regular time or when you first arrive, which is left up to you."

"Yes, ma'am."

"Terrance, you will report to the custodial office after school to meet Mr. Fleming. You will be emptying trash cans or anything else he wants you to do to help him after school. You will not be here more than one hour."

"Yes, ma'am," they answered in unison.

"Any questions?"

"No, ma'am," they answered together.

"Good. Have a great day."

"Great day, great day," Flower echoed.

Tuesday and Wednesday, Terrance and Paris had no problems with their detention assignments. Other students were surprised seeing Paris wash tables and help the cafeteria staff. Some teased her. "Where is your hair net, Paris?" "Get your glasses, you're going to need them." Paris brushed off all of the teasing because she knew this was a part of the punishment and only for one week. Next week, she would be back to her normal lunchtime and routine.

Later, Terrance was emptying trash cans with the janitorial staff and because of his strength, could take out the heavy trash bags more easily than the grown men. There weren't any students around much to tease Terrance and most of them knew why he was on detention or punishment, so they didn't mess with him much.

But on Thursday, Terrance was emptying trash cans in the classrooms on the third floor. The routine was to start on the top floor where the eighth grade students mostly had class and work his way down to the first floor and out of the door when finished. When returning a trash can to one of the classrooms, Terrance heard keys but was inside the classroom and hidden behind the door so he saw no person. He thought, *that's probably Mr. Fleming*. He ignored it at first, but with the trash can still in his hand, he heard a locker door open. He still ignored it and thought, *that's somebody who has a key lock on their locker.* He put the empty trash can on the floor and headed to the next room.

The rooms were connected in the middle, so instead of going into the hallway, Terrance went through the connecting door to the next classroom and picked up that trash can to empty it in the larger can in the hallway. Because he was behind the door, he could see the person walking down the hallway. It was Darren! Why was he on the third floor? His locker should have been on the first floor along with all of the other sixth graders.

Not wanting any more trouble than he was already in, Terrance stood behind the door watching until Darren was all the way down the stairwell and never knowing that Terrance saw him. There was no way to tell which locker Darren had been in because Terrance didn't see him until he walked by the open door. When Terrance looked at all the lockers on that part of the third floor hallway, there were no key locks on any of the lockers. He knew he heard a locker door open and close. What was Darren doing up here, and why? Did he have a master key? How did Darren get the key in the first place?

Terrance was determined to not be in any more trouble this school year. A week of detention after school was enough for him, but he had to tell Ms. Wilson, right?

Terrance kept emptying those trash cans until he arrived at the first floor, and Mr. Fleming was waiting on him.

"All done, Terrance?"

"Yes, sir."

"Great. Because you are so fast and strong, finish taking out the big bags to the dumpster. When you come back, check in with me and then you'll be done."

"Yes, sir."

When Terrance came back to the boiler room, he heard Mr. Fleming going through his key cabinet.

"I know I had four master keys, and now there are only three."

"Mr. Fleming!" Terrance called out.

"I'm here, Terrance."

"I'm done."

"All right, see you tomorrow. Two more days, and then you're done."

"I'm good. It's really not been a problem."

"Glad to hear it. You're a good boy, just made a mistake is all."

"Yes, sir, but I hope to make it right."

"You have, and you will. Goodnight, Terrance, and see you tomorrow."

"Goodnight."

Terrance paused and thought for a split second, *should I go back and tell Mr. Fleming what I heard and saw?*

He headed toward the door thinking, *I must do things the right way and tell Ms. Wilson what I saw and heard first. She will take care of it.*

The Right Way

When Terrance arrived at school the next day, he went straight to Ms. Wilson's office.

After he knocked on her door, Ms. Wilson answered, "Who is it?"

Terrance opened the door and said, "It's me, Ms. Wilson. I have something to tell you."

"I understand, Terrance, but I am on a conference call and have meetings the entire morning. Check in with me after school before you see Mr. Fleming."

"Yes, ma'am." Terrance looked down sadly as he started to shut the door.

"Terrance."

"Yes. ma'am."

"It'll be fine. Remember, you did the right thing by coming to me this morning. I promise, I'll be ready to hear everything this afternoon. Head off to class."

"Yes, ma'am."

Terrance arrived at his locker. As usual, Paris was already there.

"Hey, Terrance,"

"Hey, Paris," Terrance said quietly.

"You okay?"

"Yes."

"No, you're not. What's going on?"

"You promise not to tell?" Terrance insisted.

"I promise. Oh my goodness, what is it?" Paris asked.

"Shh, listen," Terrance said, then he began to tell Paris everything that he had seen yesterday on the third floor.

"That's terrible, Terrance."

"I know."

"Did you tell Ms. Wilson yet?"

"I tried, but she is busy this morning. I'll see her this afternoon."

"Well, be sure to tell her right away."

"I will, but, Paris, don't do anything crazy based on what I said, okay?"

"I won't, but you know I'm going to be looking at him strangely today."

"I know. I probably shouldn't have said anything, but I had to tell somebody. I didn't tell my parents last night, either."

"I'm glad you told me. Remember, we're a team."

"Really?"

"Really."

"Well, as a member of Terrance's team, I hope that you will continue to back me up, because I am tired of this bully."

"Me too. I hope he can finally be caught and we can get back to 6th grade normal."

"Whatever that is."

"Exactly."

"See you in homeroom."

"Yep."

They both went their separate ways to the same homeroom. Paris always had to make a quick stop to check out her hair in the girls' bathroom, and Terrance always went straight to homeroom, to hopefully avoid any trouble.

The morning classes went okay and things were going along as normal until lunchtime.

Paris was in the cafeteria, as usual, cleaning tables and trays, but Darren walked in and she went on high alert. She watched his every move. She probably shouldn't have, but she put on her special glasses. She told herself, *I'm not going to do anything without permission, just watch. That is all.*

He looked normal while laughing and joking with the people at the lunch table. But when he stood up to take his tray to the trash, someone bumped into him. Darren yelled, "Hey, watch where you're going!" There was a slight jingling noise because some keys fell out of his jacket pocket. Paris looked down at the keys and one said, 'master' on it. She thought, *that must be the master key Mr. Fleming is looking for.*

Paris realized at that moment that she should say something or do something right? She had promised Terrance, Ms. Wilson, and herself that she wouldn't do anything without telling Ms. Wilson or another adult. It was so hard not to approach Darren right then and there, because she knew what she had seen with her own two eyes, but he had gotten away with so much, she knew that she had to do it the right way.

Terrance had last lunch so he would see Paris in the cafeteria.

Terrance sat down with his tray and she immediately came over to his table.

"Terrance, guess what I just saw?"

"What?"

"Keys dropped out of Darren's jacket and one said 'master' on it. You think that's Mr. Fleming's key?"

"I don't know, Paris, and we can't go searching him like the police."

"True, but I can go to Ms. Wilson, too, after school and tell her what I saw."

"Sure, but aren't you going to miss your bus?"

"No, I have debate club after school."

"Okay, I guess I'll meet you in her office later."

"I guess you will."

Suddenly, Mrs. Davies approached them and said, "Excuse me, Paris, tables and trays, my dear."

"Yes, ma'am. Duty calls."

"See you later," Terrance said.

After lunch, two more class periods and then off to see Ms. Wilson.

They both arrived at Ms. Wilson's office and told her the whole story.

"First, let me say that I am proud of you both for following the rules and telling an adult, especially telling me first about all of this."

"Well, what can we do next, Ms. Wilson?" Paris asked.

"Can we catch him if we see something?" Terrance asked.

"Are you going to search him?" Paris asked.

"Will the police be called, or will you call his parents called first?" Terrance added.

"Listen to you both, trying to become amateur detectives. Right now, we have your stories, but I have access to video of each hallway and the cafeteria. Most students don't realize that we have to keep an eye on things, but the videos are only screened by administrators, when necessary."

"Okay, so after you check the videos, what happens next?" Paris asked.

"He and his parents are notified and then the principal makes the call on what to do next."

"Great! Hopefully, he can be suspended so that we can all get peace around here."

"I know that Darren can be a handful, but he deserves an education just like everyone else. He can't be accused of something until it is proven and we have evidence. Know that we can get into serious trouble accusing students of things without proper proof. Thank you both for this information and head on to your after-school duties."

"Fine," Paris said softly as she stood up and grabbed her things.

"Goodbye," Terrance said sadly as he picked up his backpack to follow Paris.

"Listen! You both did a great job. I know you want immediate action, but action can't be taken until the proper procedures are carried out first. Off you go."

Terrance and Paris left Ms. Wilson's office.

"Hey, I'll see you on Monday," Terrance said quietly while they stood in the hallway.

"Yep, just two more days of detention and this, at least, will be over," Paris replied.

"You said that right but, Paris, I want to tell you thank you."

"For what?"

"For being my friend through all of this. You didn't have to, but you stood up for me, and with me, through this whole mess."

Paris stretched out her arms in spite of her backpack and purse and said, "I'm Paris Carter and I'm on Terrance's team."

They both laughed. While walking their separate ways, their goodbyes echoed in the hallways. Both felt just a little down about the results of telling an adult. It didn't seem like enough. It didn't seem like the bully was ever going to get his just punishment. But they knew it was the right thing to do. Doing the right thing is always right, right?

Caught

On Monday, the school day progressed as normal, visiting at lockers, homeroom, and then on to classes. There was only one day left of detention, which Terrance and Paris talked about at their lockers and hoped as well as agreed that they never wanted to experience that again.

There were only a few months left in the school year, and in the morning announcements during homeroom, Mr. Smith reminded the 6th graders that there would be a dance held in three weeks to celebrate the school year.

In the cafeteria, the room was all abuzz about the upcoming dance. Paris was busy cleaning trays and tables. Terrance was going through the line to get his lunch and sit down. Darren was at the tray line and handed his tray to Paris. "Hey, Paris, would you go to the dance with me?"

"No," Paris said as she dumped his garbage in the can and began wiping it.

"Why not? You can't be serious about that nerd Terrance."

Paris didn't respond to Darren but kept emptying and wiping the next student's tray.

"Did you hear what I just said?"

"Yes, I heard you, but I choose to not respond."

"Oh, I see how it is."

Paris was calm and still didn't respond.

Terrance saw the whole thing and knew that Paris could handle herself, but he was getting angrier by the moment. Instead of stepping to Darren and causing a scene, he just stayed in his seat, trying to eat while keeping his eye on Paris the whole time. Fortunately, Darren walked away from Paris and headed for the door.

As Darren headed toward the door, Mr. Smith and Mr. Fleming came in the cafeteria and were walking down the center aisle between the two sections of table. They were walking in the same direction as Darren but never called out his name. Instead of just walking out the door, Darren turned around and started running in the opposite direction from the main front door to the side door where Terrance was sitting.

Mr. Smith, the principal, then called out Darren's name, "Darren, stop running and come back here!"

Darren didn't stop running but was headed between the tables where Terrance was sitting. Terrance stood and, with people sitting, food and chairs, with his strength, pulled the two tables together to block Darren from running out the side door. Darren was wedged between two tables of people and food flew everywhere.

The students at the table were not happy about the spills, but the students around the cafeteria cheered, "Go, Terrance go!" In front of the whole cafeteria, Darren, for once, had finally gotten caught

Paris had her special glasses on and yelled, "Mr. Smith, be sure to check his pockets," never stopping her motion of wiping off a tray.

"Students, please calm down and finish your lunch so that you can be fueled for the rest of your learning day." Turning to Terrance and Paris, the principal said, "Thank you, Terrance and Paris."

To the students at the table, Mr. Smith said, "If you students have any damage to your clothing, go to Ms. Wilson for replacements."

Mr. Taylor, the security guard, suddenly came through the side door. "I'm sorry, Mr. Smith, but I got here as fast as I could."

"No problem, Terrance Edmonds helped us. We will have to search Darren's pockets in front of his parents and we'll see if Mr. Fleming's master key is in his pockets."

"Darren, you come with me," Mr. Taylor said as Darren was now being escorted out of the cafeteria by all three men. The cafeteria cheered again.

"You hear my fan club back there?" Darren said, trying to crack a joke.

"I don't know about fan club, but take a look at the end of the hallway as your parents are waiting to tell you just how they feel about everything that has been going on," Mr. Smith said.

Darren and anyone else looking could see how angry Darren's parents were by the looks on their faces.

The rest of the day, the entire school, students and teachers, heard about what happened in the cafeteria.

Terrance and Paris had somehow become the heroes of the school.

While they were at their lockers prior to 7th period, slaps on the back and "thank you" were said to Terrance and Paris from students who passed by. The bully had finally been caught and now, hopefully, school could be a better place to come to each day.

"Terrance, I think you are a celebrity now," Paris said.

"Nope, just a guy who saw a chance to get it right."

"True, but everybody loves you."

"No, they don't love me as much as they love that Darren got caught."

"Exactly."

"Can I ask you something?"

"Sure."

"Molly said that Darren asked you to the dance."

"Molly the Mouth is always saying something. Did she also tell you what I said?"

"Nope, that's what I was going to ask you. What did you say?"

"I told him no."

"What would you say if I asked you?"

"Are you asking me to the dance, Terrance?"

"Oh, so you're going to make me ask you?"

"Yes," Paris said.

Terrance looked down at his feet but gathered all of his nerve and said, "Paris, I am asking you to go to the dance with me."

"Then my answer is yes."

"Thanks, see you later." Terrance's insides jumped up and down.

"See you later," Paris said with a smile.

Terrance thought he might even lose his lunch, even though that was four hours ago. Somehow he kept his cool and headed to see Mr. Fleming for detention. Once in the boiler room, he jumped up, threw his fist in the air, and yelled, "She said yes!"

Mr. Fleming asked, "Who said yes to what?"

"Paris is going to the dance with me!"

"Boy, I guess that's great, but you can't even drive."

"I don't care, Mr. Fleming. Paris is my date, and I'll figure the rest out later."

"Well, young man, take that same energy upstairs to the third floor and start emptying trash cans in the classrooms."

"Yes, sir, I'll be happy to."

"Whew. Help these children. Go, boy. You definitely look happy," Mr. Fleming said with a smile.

Terrance literally was running from room to room collecting and emptying trash cans. He didn't know what made him happier knowing that Paris was going to the dance with him or knowing that there was only one more day for detention. He slowed down for a second and thought, *Paris is going to the dance with me, but I can't dance!*

Somehow, his pace slowed down in the classrooms on the first floor. By the time Terrance got to the boiler room to get his backpack to leave, his head was hanging down and he looked so sad.

Mr. Fleming asked, "What's wrong, Terrance?"

"How can I take Paris, the most beautiful girl in the school, to a dance and I can't dance?"

"The same way every other middle schooler has all over the world. Be yourself. Remember, she said yes. Practice dancing with your mom."

"Thank you, Mr. Fleming."

"Go home, son."

"Yes, sir." Terrance felt a little better, but now he felt so nervous. It wasn't the first time it happened and certainly wouldn't be the last.

Later, when Terrance arrived home and opened the garage door, his dad was already home. He thought, *great, I can talk to Dad alone first.*

He opened the garage door and set his backpack on the table next to the door.

"Terrance, is that you?"

"Yes, sir."

"You okay?"

"No."

"Come in here."

Terrance could hear that his dad had turned off the television and was waiting for him in the family room.

"What's up, son?"

"I asked Paris to the 6th grade dance coming up in a couple of weeks."

"So what happened?"

"She said yes."

"That's good, isn't it?"

"Yes, but I don't know how to dance."

"I am not a great dancer either, son, just ask your mother. But the most important thing is that you asked Paris and she said yes. Middle school is such an awkward, uncomfortable time and such a growing experience that it will all feel weird or strange to you because it is your first time doing it. I realize that all that has happened to you with the bully, the super powers and all, 6th grade has been tough, but it's almost over. You've only got about another month of school and then we'll go somewhere fun and celebrate. How does that sound?"

"Great, but I still don't know how to dance."

"You will as soon as your mother comes home."

"That's what Mr. Fleming said."

"The plant operator?"

"Yes. Paris said yes right before detention and I was so happy until I remembered that I can't dance."

"Son, you'll be fine, just wait until your mother gets home."

Unbeknownst to Terrance or his father, his mother was listening.

"Wait until your mother gets home about what? Terrance Edmonds, are you in trouble again? If you are, I am going to have to take off that terrific and list you as trouble prone."

"No, Margaret, Terrance is not in trouble. Listen. Tell her, son."

Terrance told what happened to his mother and she said, "Is that all? Come here, boy, and I'll show you how it's done. I taught your daddy and I'll teach you too. Put on some music and let's rock and roll."

Terrance started laughing and his dad did, too.

"Mom, I don't think they call it rock and roll anymore," Terrance said.

"In this house, that's what I call it. My son is going to be one of the best dancers at that school dance. Let's dance."

They danced until dinner and then danced more after dinner.

"Son, I think it's bedtime."

"Sure, Dad. Thanks, Mom and Dad. I had so much fun learning to dance."

"We love you, too. Now goodnight," Terrance's mom said.

Terrance left the kitchen, but as he headed up the stairs, he noticed that there was a little light brightening up the hallway and also shining on the stairs. The music was suddenly slower. He came down the last two steps and peeked into the family room to see his parents slow dancing. He thought, *one day, I hope someone will love me like that.*

"Terrance Edmonds!" his mother shouted.

"Yes, ma'am. I know. I'm headed to bed," Terrance complained but heard his mother giggle. He smiled as he climbed the stairs to the top this time and turned right to go into his bedroom.

We Survived 6ᵗʰ Grade

The next day was huge because it was the final day of detention. Terrance went to school not knowing what the day would bring but confident that he would get through it.

His mother dropped him off at school just like normal, but no Darren. When he got to his locker, there were others at their lockers, but when they saw him, they patted him on the back and cheered. Terrance was shocked, smiled and just kept getting his things together for classes.

"Good morning, Terrance," Paris said just like every other day.

"Hey, Paris. How are you?" Terrance asked.

"Fine. Did you hear about Darren?"

"No, what happened? He wasn't on the stoop to tease me as usual."

"No, because his parents are taking him from this school and enrolling him in the alternative school for boys."

"Wow, that's terrible and terrific at the same time. I hear that school is very strict."

"I heard that, too, but serves him right for all he has done to terrorize this school."

"True, but he could have changed before it went this far. Teasing and bullying is one thing, but he stole keys, stole candy and who knows what all else he could have done that we don't know anything about."

"Exactly."

Over the intercom, came an announcement, "If Terrance Edmonds and Paris Carter are in the building, please head to Ms. Wilson's office."

"What did we do now?" Terrance asked out loud.

"Nothing, Terrance. We are just doing what we are supposed to do," Paris replied.

"I got everything. You ready?"

"Yes, in one second."

Terrance waited while Paris got her things together for the day, and then they headed to Ms. Wilson's office.

Paris knocked on the door and Ms. Wilson said, "Come in."

When the door opened, Terrance and Paris walked in to find Darren and his parents, along with Terrance and Paris' parents, who were already seated.

"Terrance and Paris, have a seat. According to district rules, your parents have to be here in attendance as well, for your protection." Ms. Wilson's office was large enough for all to have a seat.

Once everyone was seated and situated, Ms. Wilson continued, "I believe Darren has something to say to you both."

"I'm sorry," Darren in a very low-toned voice.

"Speak up, Darren, and tell them what you're sorry for," his father said.

"I'm sorry for everything. Teasing you, Terrance, and calling you Terrance the Terrific."

"You mean, the Terrible," Paris inserted.

"Yes, I said the Terrible. For teasing you and Paris in any way."

"Each and every day," Paris said.

"Paris, let him finish," Ms. Wilson added.

"I just think that if he is going to apologize, he needs to do it right," Paris insisted.

"My daughter is right," Ms. Carter added.

"I understand, but let Darren finish," Ms. Wilson said.

"Each and every day, I teased Terrance and Paris. Also, for stealing so much candy and Mr. Fleming's keys," Darren finally finished.

"Thank you, Darren. Terrance and Paris, here are your passes to get into class. By the clock, homeroom is over so head to 1st period. Thank you, Mr.

and Mrs. Edmonds and Ms. Carter for coming. I need to speak with Darren and his parents alone. Have a great rest of the day," Ms. Wilson said as she stood and walked toward the door.

Terrance and Paris took the passes to class and waved their parents goodbye as they headed down the opposite direction of the hallway.

"What happens now?" Paris asked Terrance.

"I don't know, but I can't believe he apologized."

"His parents didn't look happy at all."

"Would you be happy with your child?"

"Nope, but I think more than anything, I never thought I'd see the day that Darren would apologize."

"Me either. Miracles still do happen."

"At least today, a miracle happened."

"Exactly."

"See you later."

Terrance and Paris parted ways at the stairwell because they didn't have 1st period together but would see each other later on in the day.

Being that it was the last day of detention, the cafeteria ladies presented Paris with a signed apron for her to keep.

Paris replied, "Thank you for the apron, but I hope I never have to wear it again in school. It will be in my memory box forever."

The ladies all smiled and Ms. Davies said, "You're welcome, Paris. Keep it until you really need it in your own home one day."

"Yes, ma'am," Paris replied.

When Terrance saw Mr. Fleming, he told Terrance that he appreciated his help but never wanted to see him in detention again. They both laughed and Mr. Fleming added, "But you can stop by and say hello anytime, Terrance."

"Thank you so much, sir," Terrance said with his hand extended for a handshake.

The next two weeks of school were filled with turning in assignments, finishing up projects and taking exams. The reward for finishing all of their schoolwork was the school dance. Because the school was so large, each grade level had their own dance, and the 6th graders were first.

Terrance had been practicing with his mom as much as possible. He was so nervous, he could hardly concentrate on school, assignments, and the exams.

The Friday of the dance finally came. The dress wasn't formal, but Terrance's mom had shopped for a pair of dress pants and button-down shirt for him. She had put so much starch on the shirt and ironed it so much that Terrance started to scratch when he wore it.

"Stand up straight, Terrance."

"Yes, Mom."

"Margaret, you're doing too much. Stop fussing over Terrance. This is the 6th grade dance, not his wedding."

"Hey, this is my son and I do what I please."

"Oh, Mom, Dad, I'm so nervous, I feel like I'm going to throw up."

"Those are just butterflies."

"I don't know when they'll go away, but don't throw up on Paris."

"I'll try not to."

"Let's go, or we'll be late."

When they got to the kitchen and were about to head toward the garage, Terrance's mom stopped at the refrigerator and retrieved a small box. "Wait, I've got something for Terrance to give Paris."

"Oh, Mom, is that necessary?"

"Yes, it is very necessary. You are my son and I don't want you to be embarrassed at this dance. You hear?"

"Yes, ma'am."

The Edmonds got in the car and headed to the school. Paris and her mother were meeting them there.

When they walked in, Terrance's mom went over to the refreshment table. His father found a seat along the wall to sit down. Terrance looked around really quickly but didn't see Paris. She hadn't arrived yet.

Molly the Mouth walked up and asked, "Terrance, what's in the box?"

"Molly, none of your business," Terrance said as he turned around and went back to the entrance just outside the gym. His heart was beating fast, and he was starting to sweat. He thought, *this is your big moment. You can't blow it now. You've worked hard.*

You've practiced dancing and everything. No mistakes.

Just then, the outside door opened and who walked in but Paris and her mother. It looked like the light from outside made Paris look like she was glowing. Terrance didn't think he would be able to talk or even walk toward her as pretty as she looked. Instead, he stood still as she walked toward him. Her hair was even curlier than it had been at school earlier. The dress she wore was pink, with ruffles and a white bow. Terrance knew that he would never forget this moment as long as he lived. This was it.

"Hey, Terrance."

"Hey, Paris. Hey, Ms. Carter."

"Hello, Terrance."

"What's in that box?" Paris asked.

"Something for you. My mom said that you would like it. I don't know, but let me know if you don't like it," Terrance said nervously.

"Well, open it and let me see," Paris insisted.

Terrance almost dropped the box but caught it before it hit the floor.

"Don't be nervous. It's okay," Ms. Carter encouraged.

When Terrance opened the box, there was a beautiful white corsage with a wrist band to be placed on Paris' wrist.

"Oh, that's pretty,"

"I'm glad you like it."

"Let me put it on you, Paris," her mother said.

"Thanks, Mom."

When she had the corsage on, Terrance said, "You ready to go in?"

"Of course. We deserve this. We survived 6th grade, so let's celebrate."

"Yes, Terrance's Team should celebrate," Terrance said as Paris giggled.

They walked in and danced the night away. No mess ups. No mistakes. No stepping on Paris' toes. No spilled juice, just fun. A terrific ending to a somewhat tough school year.

A Note from the Author

Thank you so much for enjoying Terrance the Terrific Series #1 and his journey through the 6th grade. I hope that you enjoyed it.

Please tell your parents, teachers, or librarian to email me at bkroystonpublishing@gmail.com with any comments, thoughts, or ideas for 7th grade. We have only started and have much more to go with the Terrance Edmonds character, including Paris and a sneak peek at a new character. No name yet, but the release will come soon enough.

Let's go!

Questions for Discussion

The beauty of fiction is that as the author, I can make the characters do and say anything that I want, within reason. Tell me one thing that you know wouldn't possibly happen in your school.

How important is telling an adult when there is a problem?

What do you think should happen to Darren now that he's confessed to all of the things that he's done?

Do you think that Terrance and Paris should be able to use their super powers at all? How and why?

About the Author

Julia Royston spends her days doing what she loves, writing, publishing, speaking and coaching others to tell, introduce, and create ways to deliver their stories and messages to the world. That is her "Why." BK Royston Publishing LLC, Julia Royston.net, Royal Media and Publishing, and Royston Book Fairs are the conduits that she uses to spread the love of reading, writing books as well as build businesses around the world.

Visit http://solo.to/juliaaroyston for more information and upcoming events.

Book #1 in the Series

TERRANCE THE TERRIFIC

Julia A. Royston

Book #2 in the Series

TERRANCE THE TERRIFIC
THE TERRIBLE STEM LAB PROJECT

JULIA A. ROYSTON

Next Up?

Made in the USA
Monee, IL
07 July 2023